An Imprint of Pearson Education

201 West 103rd Street

Indianapolis, Indiana 46290

ISBN: 0-7440-0295-8

Printing Code: The rightmost double-digit
number is the year of the book's printing; the
rightmost single-digit number is the number of
the book's printing. For example, 03-1 shows
that the first printing of the book occurred
in 2003.

06 05 04 03   4 3 2 1

Manufactured in the United States of America.

CONTENTS

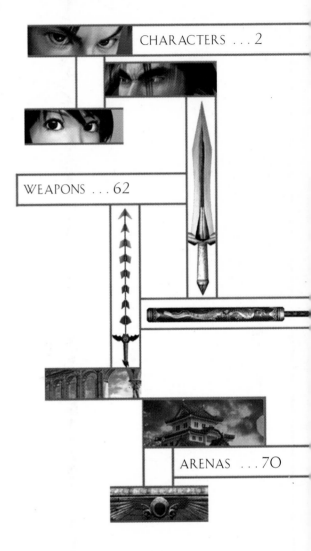

BradyGAMES Staff

Publisher	David Waybright
Editor-In-Chief	H. Leigh Davis
Marketing Manager	Janet Eshenour
Creative Director	Robin Lasek
Licensing Manager	Mike Degler
Assistant Marketing Manager	Susie Nieman

Credits

Project Editor	Christian Sumner
Senior Project Editor	Ken Schmidt
Lead Book Designer	Carol Stamile
Book Designers	Chris Luckenbill Ann-Marie Deets

CERVANTES
セルバンテス

Under the influence of Soul Edge, the dread pirate Cervantes slaughtered his entire crew and fed off of the souls of swordsmen who dared to challenge him. One day, a warrior destroyed one of the demonic blades and defeated Cervantes. However, the pieces of Soul Edge buried in his body resurrected him. Cervantes sought the fragments of the sword, only to realize that the second sword had been shattered as well. He picked up several pieces of the newly created shards and gazed upon them. His ultimate goal was the revival of Soul Edge. And for that, he needed as many fragments of the evil blade as he could find.

MITSURUGI

御剣 平四郎

HEISHIRO MITSURUGI

Born into a peasant family, Mitsurugi became a renowned mercenary, earning nick-names such as "One Man Army" and "Demon." After hearing a story of the Soul Edge, he set out in search for it. Four years into his search, Mitsurugi visited a castle near the Ming frontier where a mysterious man handed him a piece of Soul Edge.

HEISHIRO MITSURUGI

NIGHTMARE
ナイトメア

Originally the leader of a group of brigands known as the Schwarzwind (Black Wind), Siegfried Schtauffen left to find Soul Edge after his father was murdered. Eventually he won the Soul Edge, which spoke to him, saying that if he used the souls absorbed by the sword, he could resurrect his father. From that moment on, he became Nightmare, the evil knight who struck fear into every corner of Europe. Three years later, his dream was crushed when a warrior wielding a spirit sword called Soul Calibur appeared. Nightmare was defeated, but he managed to survive and regained some of his sanity. Along with lucidity came the horrifying memories of the sins he committed, and the realization that he had murdered his father. After four years, he was once again Nightmare, his body taken over by Soul Edge completely.

NIGHTMARE

TAKI

多喜

After defeating the dread pirate Cervantes, Taki attempted to fuse a fragment of Soul Edge she removed from Sophitia's body into the demonic blade, Mekki-Maru. Much to her surprise, Mekki-Maru began to surge with even more evil energy. She searches for Soul Edge, hoping to destroy both swords by pitting them against one another.

TAKI

SEUNG MINA

成美那

SEUNG MI NA

Seung Mina began training with the zanbatou at an early age and grew to be a skilled warrior. Her first attempt to find the Soul Edge was cut short by Hwangdmdha student at her family's dojo. When a second student from the dojo, Yun Sung, left with a family heirloom, Seung Mina took it upon herself to return with both, and to resume her search for the Soul Edge.

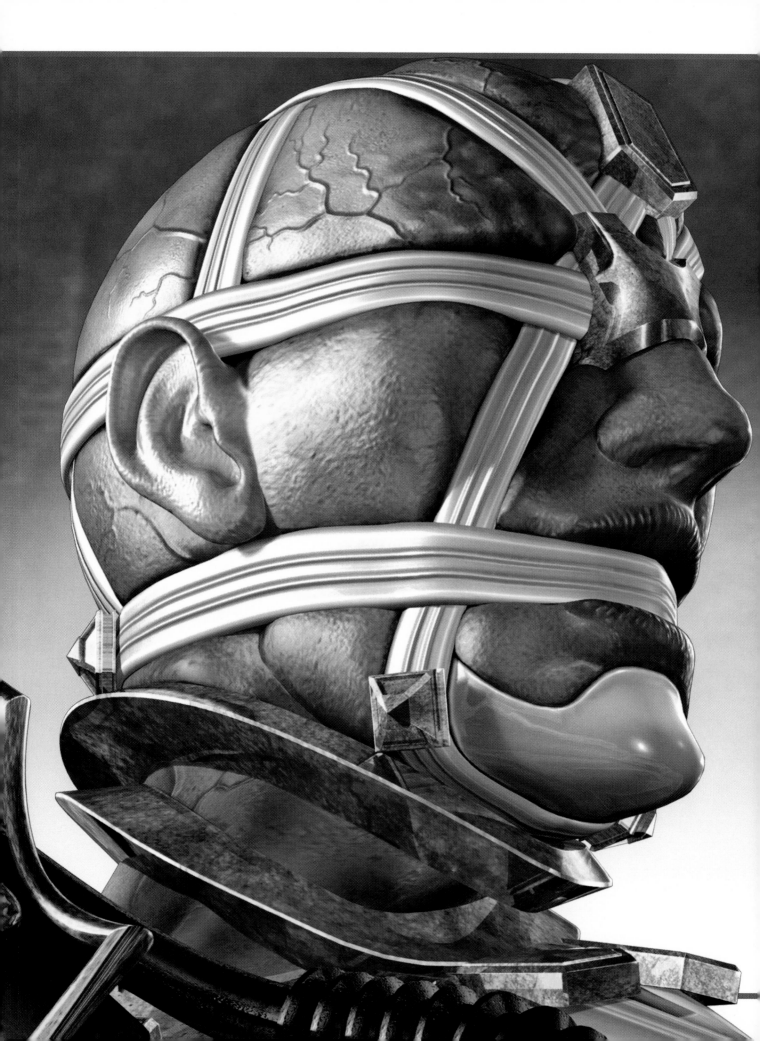

VOLDO
ヴォルド

Voldo guarded the Money Pit for Vercci, the Italian "Merchant of Death". One day after Voldo chased away a female intruder, he heard his long-lost master's voice ordering him to follow the Soul Edge's aura emanating from her sword. Voldo eventually returned with a sword with a strange aura. Four years passed before Voldo realized the sword he brought back was not Soul Edge, but he knew the truth would be revealed if he searched for the weapon once more.

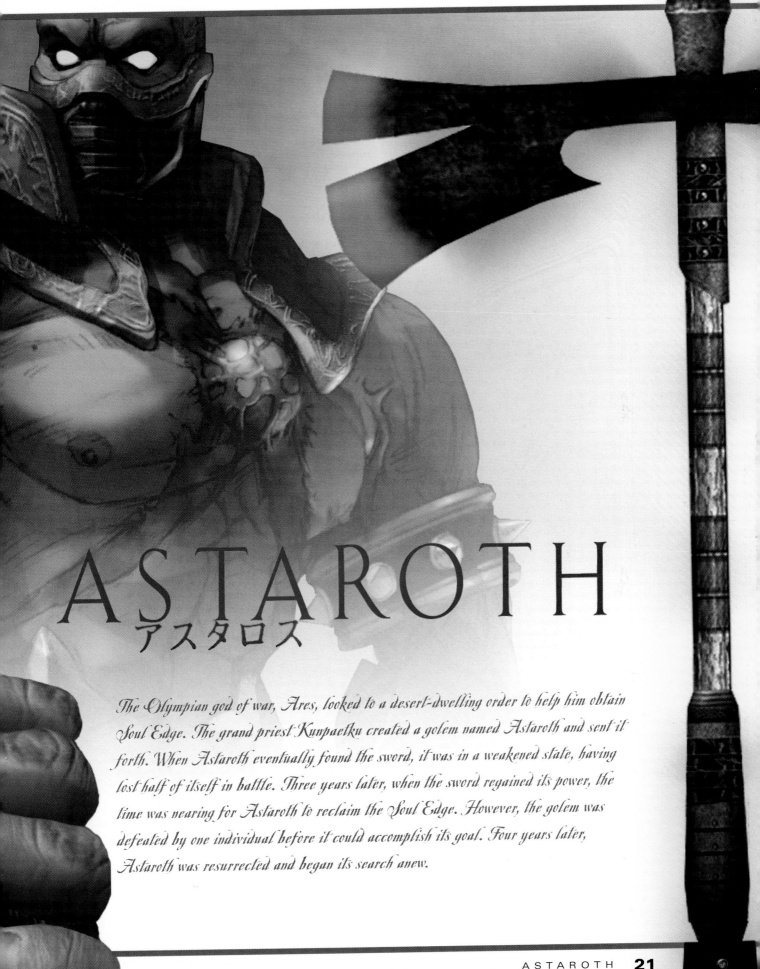

ASTAROTH
アスタロス

The Olympian god of war, Ares, looked to a desert-dwelling order to help him obtain Soul Edge. The grand priest Kunpaetku created a golem named Astaroth and sent it forth. When Astaroth eventually found the sword, it was in a weakened state, having lost half of itself in battle. Three years later, when the sword regained its power, the time was nearing for Astaroth to reclaim the Soul Edge. However, the golem was defeated by one individual before it could accomplish its goal. Four years later, Astaroth was resurrected and began its search anew.

ASTAROTH

IVY
アイヴィー

ISABELLA VALENTINE

Ivy's adopted father, Count Valentine, was driven insane by his pursuit of Soul Edge. By the time of his death, the Valentines—one of London's most distinguished families—were in ruins. Obeying the wishes of her adoptive father, Ivy continued the search for Soul Edge. She vowed to destroy Soul Edge to avenge her father's death.

ISABELLA VALENTINE

KILIK
キリク

Kilik was to be the successor of one of the sacred treasures of Ling-Sheng Su Temple, called Kali-Yuga. Tragically, the night before the succession ceremony, a mysterious light fell upon the temple, driving all those who saw it into a murdering frenzy. Kilik was no exception, and he killed many temple members. An old hermit revealed that the root of this evil was the Soul Edge. Kilik studied the art of the Ling-Sheng Su style rod and left on a journey to destroy the evil blade.

KILIK

MAXI
真喜志

Maxi, the pirate from Ryukyu, led a carefree life on the high seas until an encounter with Kilik led to his crew being slaughtered by a horde of monsters. Avenging his crew ended with an encounter with Astaroth and Ares, the god of war. The injuries Maxi sustained during the encounter ended his wanderlust, but four years later, he was drawn to rumors of a man with a gigantic ax.

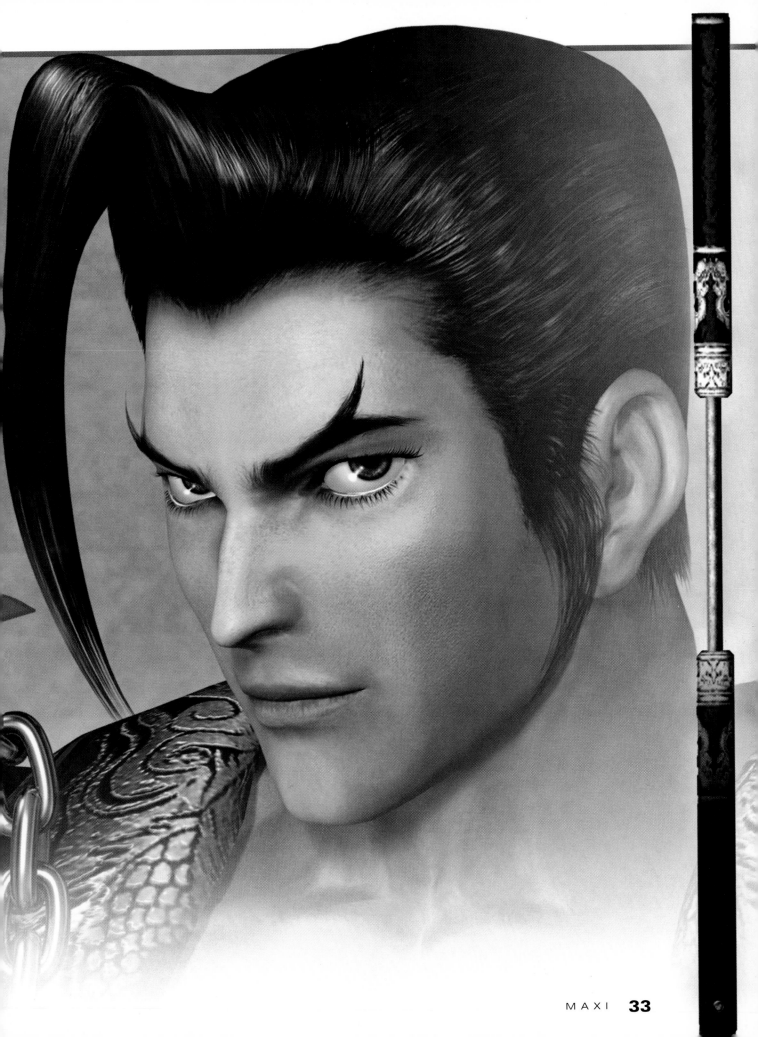

SOPHITIA
ソフィーティア

SOPHITIA ALEXANDRA

Sophitia was the eldest daughter of a baker. Her life was rather ordinary until the day Hephaestus, the god of fire and forge, ordered her to destroy an evil sword called Soul Edge. She shattered half of the sword, and later learned that someone else destroyed the other half. The appearance of a mysterious metal fragment set her on a quest to save her family.

XIANGHUA

柴香華

CHAI XIANGHUA

Xianghua, a member of the royal guard, was assigned to a mission to find the Soul Edge, a mission that was thought to have failed. In truth, Xianghua destroyed the sword after learning of its true nature. Xianghua heard rumors of Soul Edge fragments that existed, so she felt she must find every single fragment and crush them down until nothing remained!

CHAI XIANGHUA

YOSHIMITSU
吉光

Yoshimitsu, the sole survivor of a ninja clan that was massacred, traveled across the sea following the rumors of an ultimate weapon. Four years passed before Yoshimitsu infiltrated a tomb where he found his once-lost katana, along side a metal fragment that emanated the same evil energy as his blade. If there were other things that possessed the same evil energy within, it was up to him to find them and rid them from this world.

CASSANDRA
カサンドラ

CASSANDRA ALEXANDRA

It was seven years earlier that Cassandra witnessed Taki bring Sophitia home, and draw out shards of the Soul Edge out of her sister's flesh. When Sophitia disappeared again a few years later, Cassandra was certain that her sister had left to contend with Soul Edge once more. She realized then that Soul Edge was still alive, but she could not allow her sister to carry the burden any longer.

CASSANDRA ALEXANDRA

CHARADE
シャレード

The man's life was far from glorious, but he heard a story of *Soul Edge*, the ultimate weapon. He bought metal fragments he believed were pieces of *Soul Edge*, and kept them safe. But that was a fateful mistake as the fragments did not keep him safe from bandits that slew him and threw the corpse down a ravine. Months passed, and the pieces of metal in the man's grasp disappeared over time. The only thing left behind were trails of something that had crawled around.

NECRID
ネクリッド

Necrid was a warrior that managed to reach Soul Edge. The energy of the evil blade poisoned his body, and the warrior's mind and body became something other than human. A bloodthirsty abomination, Necrid sought the one thing that gave solace to his constant pain—the fragments of Soul Edge. His only thought was to collect every piece he could find.

RAPHAEL
ラファエル

Raphael grew up with the rapier and medicine as his playmates. His cool demeanor created many enemies, but his quick decision-making and execution skills solidified his family amongst the nobles. Unfortunately, Raphael was cast out one day when he made a critical mistake. After the kindness of a young villager named Amy saved Raphael, he discovered a letter with references to the Soul Edge. What if such a sword was thrust into the hands of the nobles? It would all be worth it if the petty nobles could be eliminated, securing a meaningful future for Amy. But in order to accomplish his goal, Raphael needed Soul Edge; he was determined to obtain the sword by any means necessary.

RAPHAEL SOREL

TALIM
タリム

Talim was the daughter of a village's shamans, and was raised to become the last priestess. One day, as Talim read the winds as she had done many times, an evil aura surged into her body. Talim lost consciousness and did not wake for days. Soon after, Talim left the village. She sensed the resonance of the same evil aura from other parts of the world. She realized that everything would be consumed if the evil force continued to spread. Talim knew she had to find all of the fragments and seek their rightful place.

TALIM

YUNSUNG

洪潤星

Hong Yun Sung

As a boy, Yun Sung entered the Seung dojo where he grew to be a reckless young man. In order to prove himself, Yun Sung wished to fight Hwang Sung Kyung—a man who had traveled the world twice in his search for the "Sword of Salvation." Hwang, once Yun Sung's idol, declined Yun Sung's challenges for he had grown wiser during his journeys and had other priorities. Yun Sung eventually understood the foolishness of challenging someone for personal reasons, but what could he do to make Hwang acknowledge him? He realized that if he could obtain the Sword of Salvation, Hwang would be forced to recognize his talents and respect him.

HONG YUNSUNG

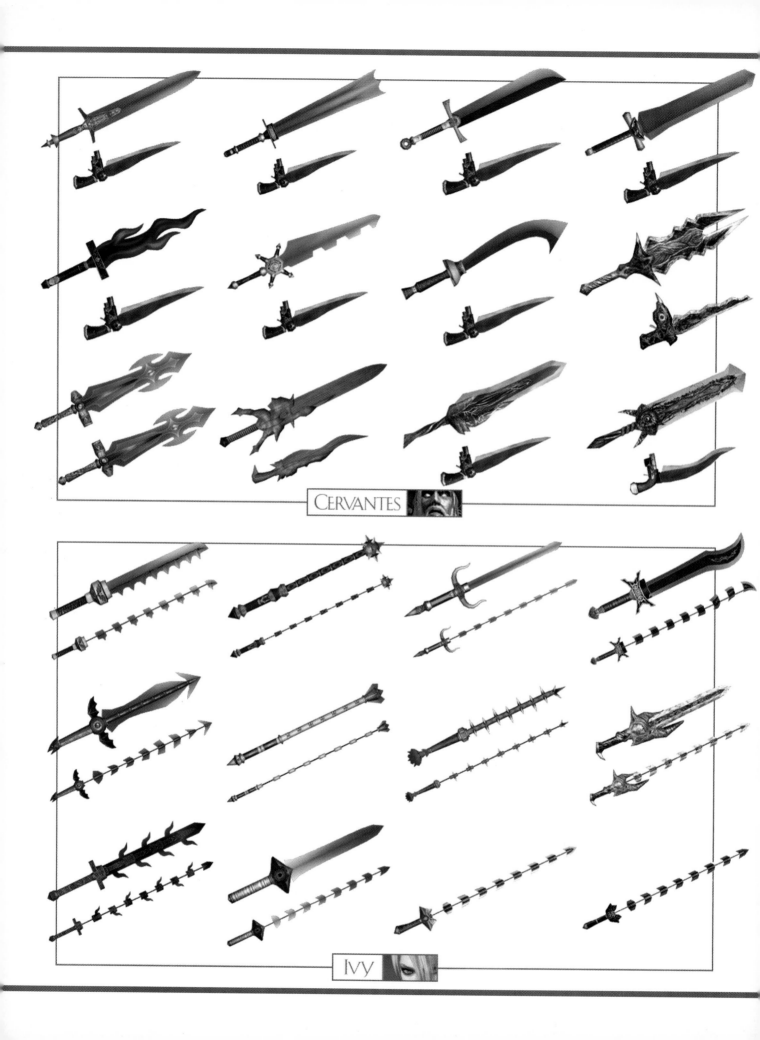

CERVANTES

IVY

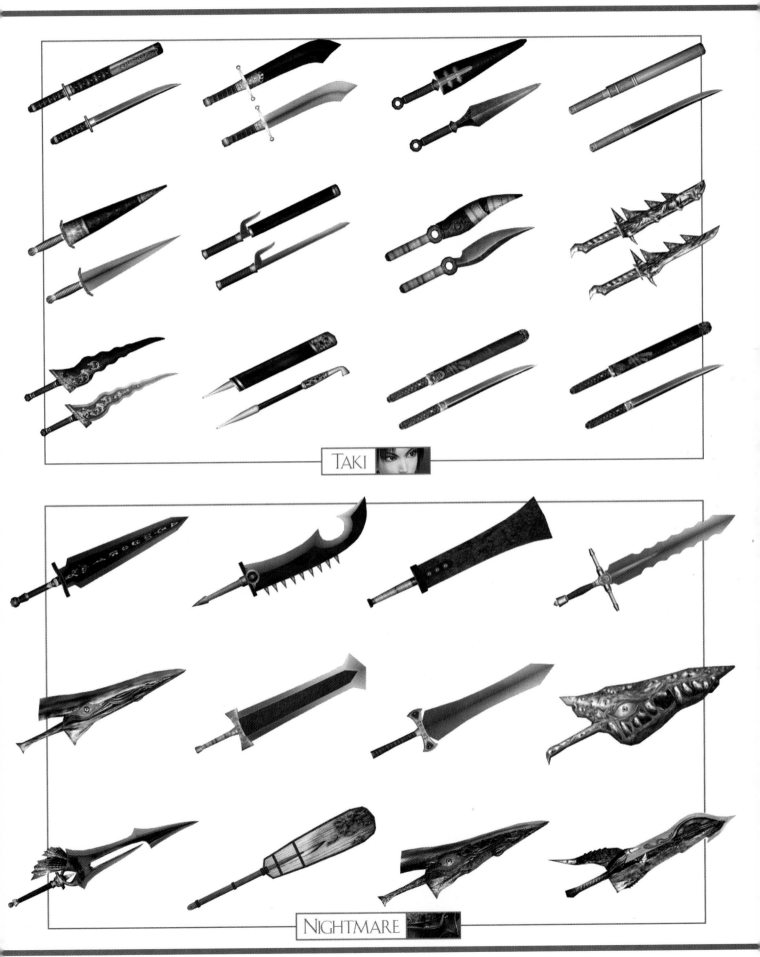

TAKI

NIGHTMARE

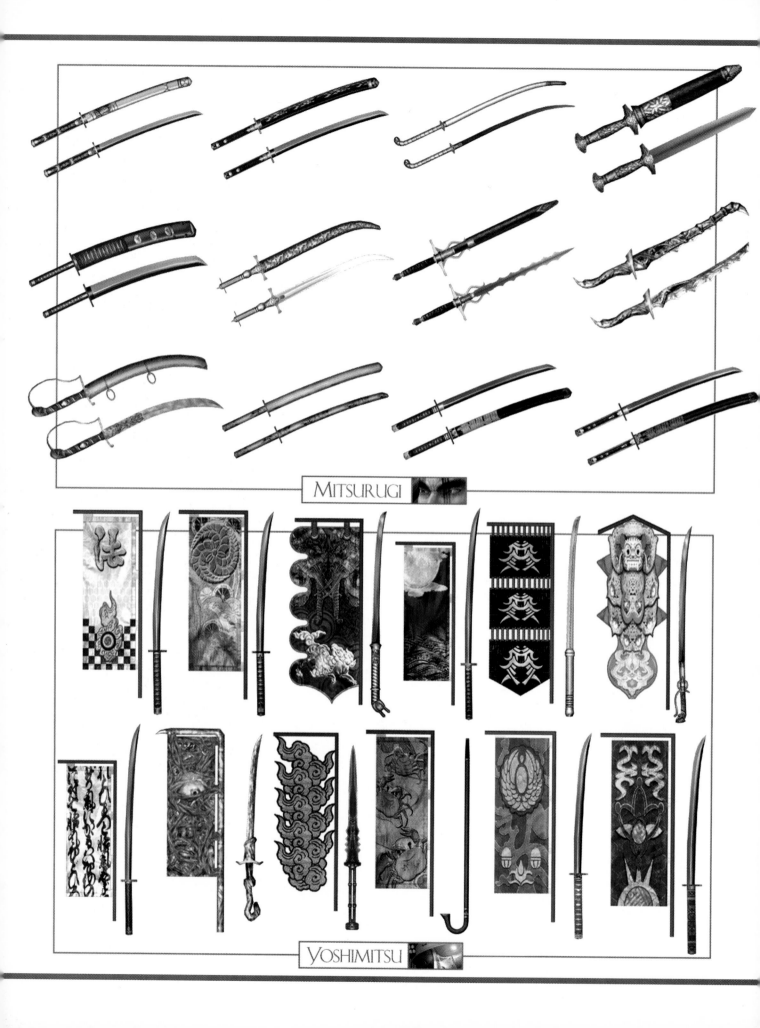

MITSURUGI

YOSHIMITSU

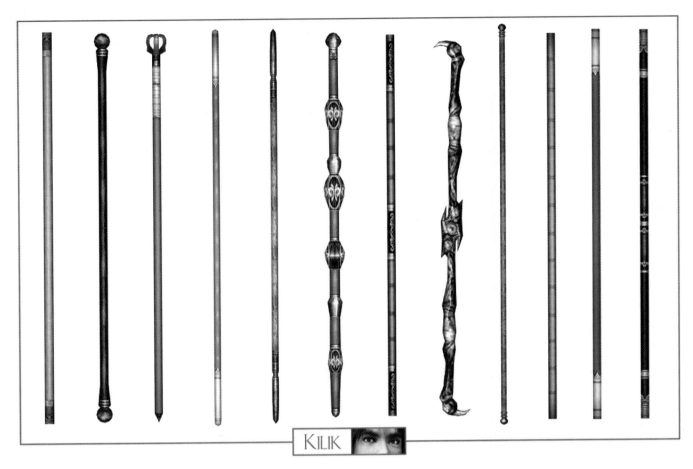

KILIK

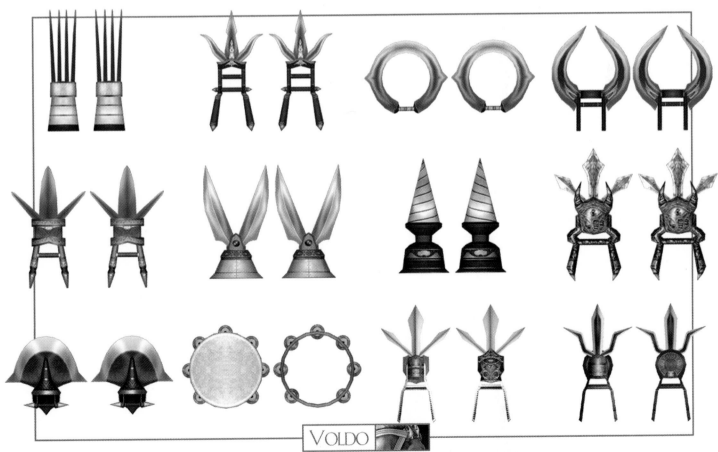

VOLDO

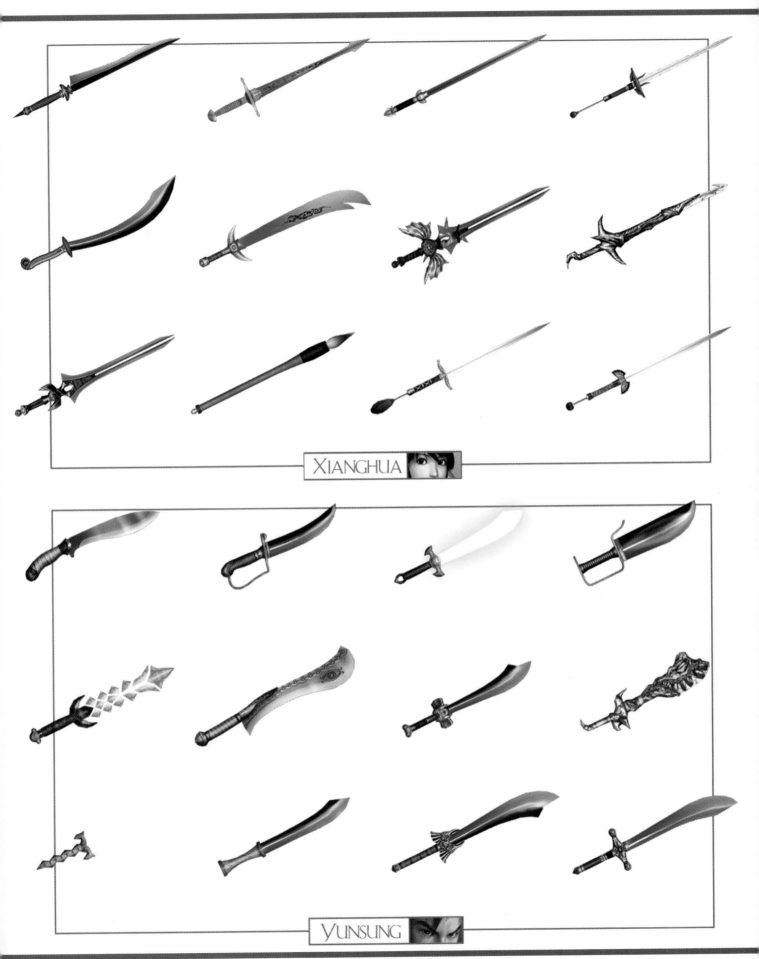

XIANGHUA

YUNSUNG

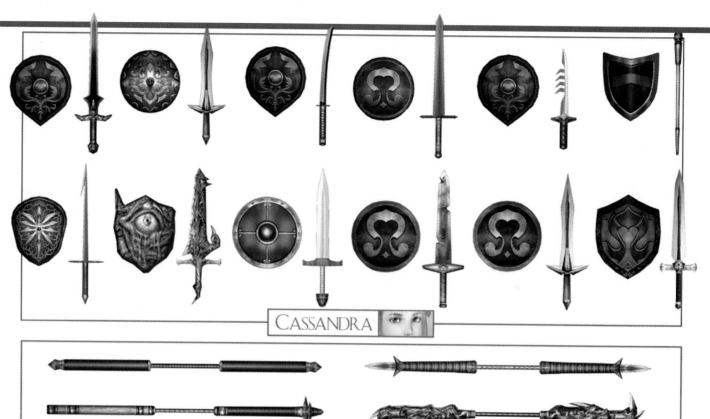

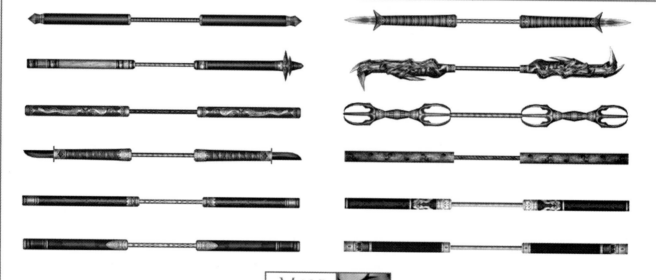

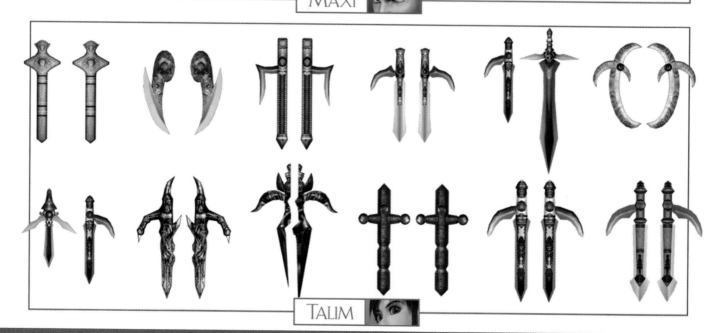

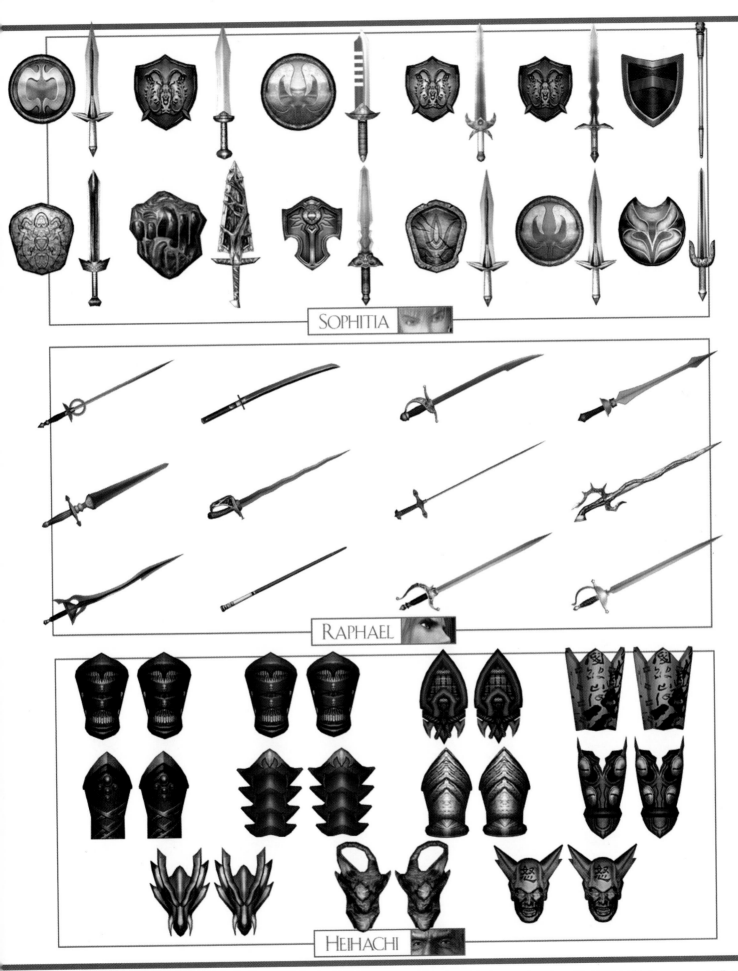

SOPHITIA

RAPHAEL

HEIHACHI

OSTRHEINSBURG CHAPEL

EURYDICE SHRINE GALLERY

IMPERIAL CAPITAL AYUTTHAYA

PALGAEA SHRINE/LOWEST LEVEL

MONEY PIT/TOP TIER

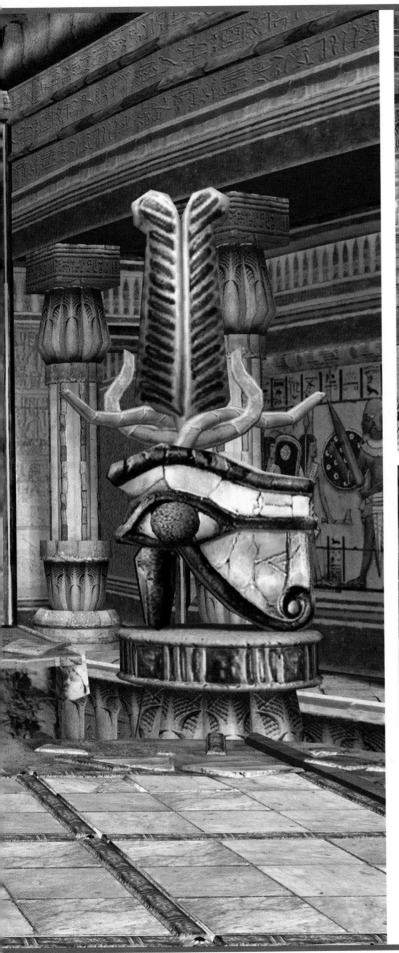

EGYPTIAN RUINS

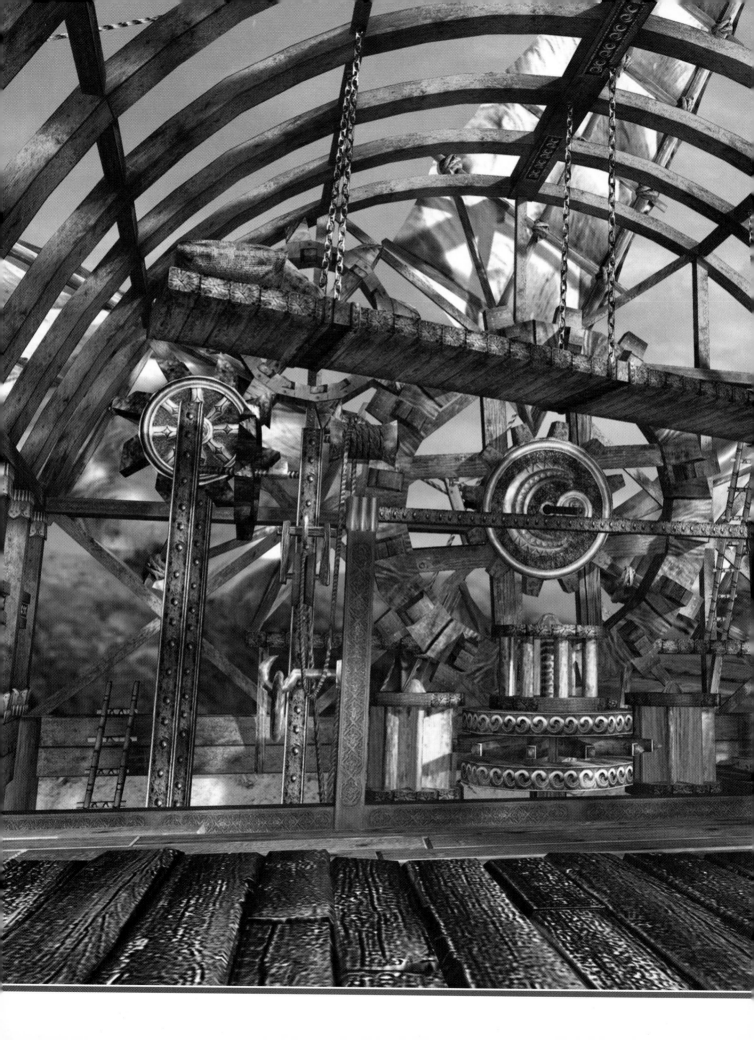

VILLAGE OF THE WIND

PIRATES' ALCOVE

KAMINOI CASTLE
SAKURA-DAI GATE

HWANGSEO PALACE
PHOENIX COURT

LABYRINTH

LAKESIDE COLISEUM

**SOUTH FRANCE
MANSION LIBRARY**

XIWEI SIEGE RUINS

TARTAROS

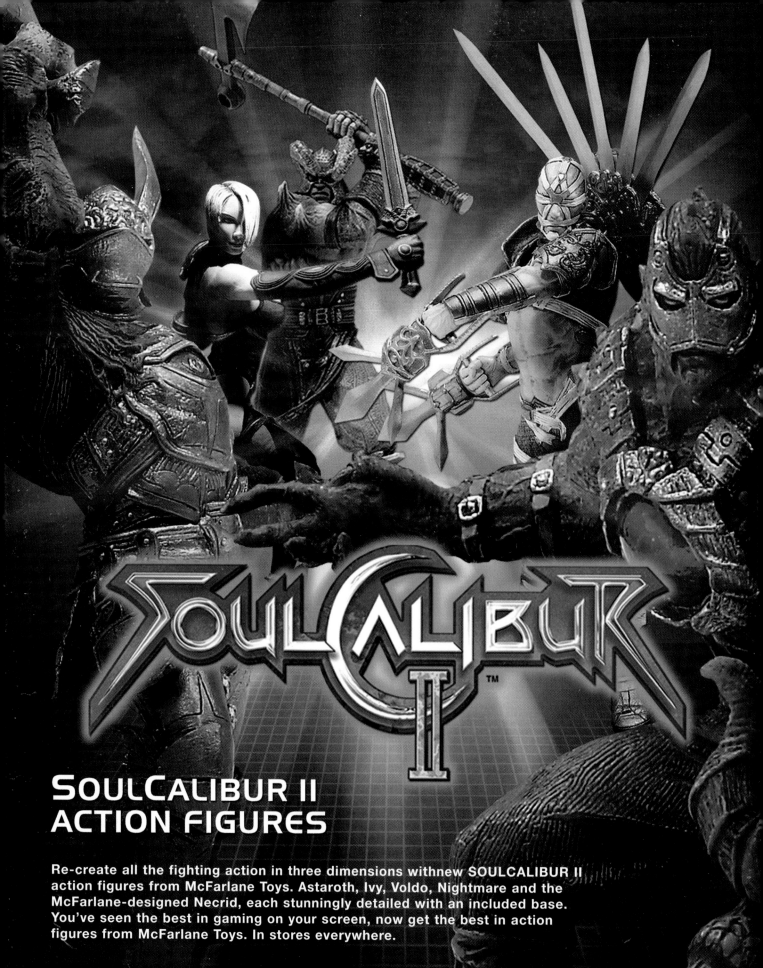

SOULCALIBUR II
ACTION FIGURES

Re-create all the fighting action in three dimensions with new SOULCALIBUR II action figures from McFarlane Toys. Astaroth, Ivy, Voldo, Nightmare and the McFarlane-designed Necrid, each stunningly detailed with an included base. You've seen the best in gaming on your screen, now get the best in action figures from McFarlane Toys. In stores everywhere.

SPAWN.COM **MCFARLANE TOYS** IT'S AN ATTITUDE